THE SKYE SCENE

DESCRIBED AND PHOTOGRAPHED
BY
ERIC G. MEADOWS

OLIVER AND BOYD
EDINBURGH: TWEEDDALE COURT
LONDON: 98 GREAT RUSSELL ST., W.C.

FIRST PUBLISHED - - - 1951

PRINTED IN GREAT BRITAIN BY
OLIVER AND BOYD LTD., TWEEDDALE COURT, EDINBURGH

PREFACE

SOME of the most wildly dramatic scenery in the British Isles is to be found in the Isle of Skye, and, throughout the years, numberless people have come under its spell. In their various ways, many artists have sung its praises, and, in recent years, the unique mountains in particular have received full tribute.

But the island possesses other features of striking beauty and grandeur that will fascinate the visitor—the strange moorlands, stupendous sea-cliffs, storm-beaten headlands, sea-lochs, ancient fortresses and scattered crofting hamlets. All these I have endeavoured to portray in this book, and I trust it may succeed in giving the reader a true impression of the atmosphere of the island with its ever-changing moods.

It may perhaps interest photographers to know that my cameras were a Rolleiflex and a ¼-plate Sanderson with normal, wide-angle and long-focus lenses; my preference being for the larger camera whenever possible. I used both orthochromatic and panchromatic films, together with a light yellow filter on most occasions.

I am indebted to the Controller of H.M. Stationery Office for permission to reproduce the simplified map that is based upon the Ordnance Survey. The Ordnance Survey spelling has been generally adopted where, as is common, there are variations in the spelling of place and feature names, and the most appropriate meanings are given where their derivation is uncertain.

LUTON, *August*, 1950   E. G. M.

CONTENTS

9

CONTENTS

CONTENTS

CONTENTS

INTRODUCTION

THE Isle of Skye, with a land area of some 670 square miles (including its own lesser islands), is the second largest Hebridean island. It is separated from the mainland of Scotland at the nearest point by a mere third of a mile of water.

To anyone who does not know the island or the nearby mainland, it may seem to consist of almost endless stretches of barren moorland and bare, rocky heights rising to rain-bearing cloud. Again there may only dimly be discerned, through the all-enveloping mist and rain, a succession of sour peat bogs on a rough moor, with occasionally a few bare dwellings that only make one wonder how anyone can live there. What is it that makes Skye so dear to the hearts of countless numbers who know it, and stirs them as they read the touching lament of the Canadian exiles in the last century:—

> From the lone shieling of the misty island
> Mountains divide us, and the waste of seas—
> Yet still the blood is strong, the heart is Highland,
> And we in dreams behold the Hebrides!
> Fair these broad meads, these hoary woods are grand;
> But we are exiles from our father's land.

What draws so many from far and wide to visit and revisit its shores, and leaves them with such a deep longing to know more of it? It is hoped the answer will be found in the following pages.

For many people, the hills and mountains are the island's chief attraction. Foremost among them are the unique and dominating Cuillin (alternatively Cuillins or Coolins), carved from a domed

13

mass of hard igneous rock called gabbro. Their bare and precipitous slopes rise above green moorland to a series of frost-sculptured ridges and acute peaks—a rock climber's paradise. Between the ridges, deep hollows or corries have been cut by Ice Age glaciers. Some of these rock amphitheatres are hanging valleys with small lochs, like Coire Lagan with its ice-smoothed floor of solid rock. Coir' a' Ghrunnda has a number of platforms like gigantic steps, with a loch on the highest one.

Though little over 3,000 feet in height, the Cuillin rival many greater mountains in grandeur and apparent size. This is due to their steepness, the compactness of their jagged peaks and the ever-changing atmospheric effects. In dry, frosty weather between the winter's long periods of rain and gales, the extremely clear atmosphere makes them stand out in sharp outline. Beyond a snow-dappled foreground of soft greens and browns, the snowy peaks rise towards a canopy of dark clouds. As the short day closes, the snow becomes tinged with pink, deepening to crimson and changing later to rose; finally fading to a wan grey against the darkening sky. In other seasons at dawn or sunset, the grey rocks, bathed in the sun's rays, may appear like glowing embers, while the hollows lie in deep shadow.

At night, these mountains may have an unearthly appearance when silhouetted against the glow of the aurora borealis; or by moonlight with snow on their peaks, they look almost like lunar mountains, cold and deserted.

Sometimes the heights seem to be eternally shrouded in mist. Sheets of rain may lash the moors all day, but in the evening the westering sun pierces the gloom, suffusing the mist and low cloud with vivid yellow, while the heavy cloud above is indigo-grey and deep violet. Fleeting glimpses may be had of dark rock and detached pinnacles behind veils of dissolving mist. The wind that has roared among the crags all day has now dropped to a gentle

14

breeze, and the only sound is that of falling waters in a thousand streams and rivulets.

From any of the Cuillin tops Skye is spread out map-like, dotted near the coast with white-walled cottages, and houses even in Uig, 25 miles away, may be visible to the unaided eye. The weather perhaps is very quiet with the sea every shade of blue. A thin pearly haze fills the distant atmosphere, through which the Outer Isles, reposing in the western deep, are blue-grey and softened in outline. Beyond them, two faint forms represent St. Kilda, 95 miles away. A few ravens occasionally circle the peaks, and glide over the ridges extended below like the backbone and limbs of a gigantic monster. Only the harsh croak of these birds, the murmur of streams in the corries and sometimes the rustle of scree sound upon the tranquil air. South-westward the sea is shimmering silver, crossed by darker lanes of unruffled water. There, lie the Isles of Eigg, Muck, Rhum and Canna. To the east, over the sun-baked Red Hills, rise a host of peaks on the mainland that extend in unbroken array to the Paps of Jura, nearly 100 miles distant. Truly this panorama is magnificent in its vastness.

In the very heart of the Cuillin is the Coruisk Basin with its sullen loch, around which dark walls of rock tower to riven ridges and shattered peaks. These walls seem to form a continuous naked cliff, with here and there long smooth slabs where intrusive sills, having the same inclination, rest upon the gabbro. The lower slopes have been steepened, smoothed and rounded by the mighty Ice-Age glacier that gouged out the Basin. Nowhere in the British Isles is the effect of glaciation more pronounced. At the seaward end of the loch the smoothed rock spreads out in vast unbroken undulations and rises for hundreds of feet, in dramatic contrast to the roughness of the higher crags. Lumps of stone carried along in the ice have scored the rock of its bed, and gigantic boulders transported on the surface of the glacier still lie where they were stranded when the ice melted.

15

Many people have been to the shores of Loch Coruisk since Sir Walter Scott visited it on a murky day, and later described it in his " Lord of the Isles," in which he makes Bruce exclaim :

> A scene so rude, so wild as this
> Yet so sublime in barrenness,
> Ne'er did my wandering footsteps press,
> Where'er I happ'd to roam.

The loch is certainly seen best in stormy or lowering weather, but even in sunshine, though the gloominess has gone, the stern grandeur of the scene remains.

After the dark, splintered Cuillin, the almost unbroken slopes of the neighbouring Red Hills may seem featureless except as a contrast. Their outlines, however, are more restful, with smooth domes, pyramids and steep ridges. In origin they are akin to the Cuillin, for they are the remnants of a vast granite intrusion into the surface basalts towards the end of the period of igneous activity. Adjoining these granitic hills is Blaven, one of the most picturesque mountains in Scotland. Shattered precipices below its cleft summit, and the Clach Glas ridge on the north, produce mountain form of rare grandeur. This form has stirred the hearts of thousands, including Alexander Smith, who wrote :

> O Blaavin, rocky Blaavin,
> How I long to be with you again,
> To see lashed gulf and gulley
> Smoke white in the windy rain—
> To see in the scarlet sunrise
> The mist wreaths perish with heat,
> The wet rock slide with a trickling gleam
> Right down to the cataract's feet, . . .

In north-east Skye, the promontory of Trotternish has a backbone ridge with hump-backed heights. Rounded, grassy slopes roll down to the west, but on the east side an escarpment of basaltic crags towers above peaty moorland. The traverse of this ridge is one of the finest walks in the island on a clear day. For a time these

16

high hills are a peaceful retreat from the sight of man and most of his works. Overhead the clouds may drift across the blue, or perhaps gather in angry masses, to break in sudden showers of rain or hail that quickly pass. The buffeting wind in the grass, the bleating of sheep or the whirr of frightened wings are the only sounds. Heavy clouds, with their edges torn into great white plumes, trail sheets of hail over distant mountains. These squalls soon disperse, to reveal dark peaks sprinkled white. Westward on the horizon are the clear-cut outlines of the Outer Hebrides.

The highest summit on the Trotternish ridge is Beinn Storr. Below walls of dark rock on its eastern face, numbers of rock pinnacles crown steep mounds of fine, mossy turf. The largest is the Old Man, about 150 feet high and a prominent landmark. Far below this rock spire are Lochs Leathan and Fada, like jewels in the green valley, with the even slopes of the Red Hills and the serrated outline of the Cuillin dominating the skyline to the south. In the Sound is low Rona with its series of rocky hillocks, and above the farther shore are the great Torridon mountains.

Near the northern end of the Trotternish escarpment are turreted crags and rock needles, above grassy hollows and knolls capped with tors, similar to those on Beinn Storr. All these weird rock forms are the result of vast landslides, due to the instability of the limestone foundations. Among the riven precipices is the Quirang, a large depression with steep sides, having in its centre—the Table— a mass of rock, capped with a level lawn of the finest turf, that has sunken over 400 feet into this hollow. From here, down clefts between great rock bastions, the moors can be seen far below with fertile fields near the coast. Over expanses of sea rise the dim mainland mountains.

Throughout the island are many lesser, but fine, moorland hills, the highest remnants of the eroded basalt plateau that constitutes most of Skye. Characteristic of them are long slopes of bright

green grass, heather and bracken, broken by continuous bands or sills of protruding rock that sometimes form flat summits. Probably the finest of these hills are MacLeod's Tables (Healaval Mor and Beag). Minginish has a number of moorland hills with a quiet charm all their own, partly due to their loneliness and to the strangeness of their structure. Many of them are excellent vantage points for the western Cuillin. Talisker is dominated by Preshal Mor, a noble hill with very rugged upper slopes that add greatly to its grandeur and apparent height. Boswell climbed this hill during his tour with Dr. Johnson. He writes in his Journal : " After dinner he (Col) and I walked to the top of Prieshwell, a very high rocky hill, from whence there is a view of Barra,—the Long Island,—Bernera,—the Loch of Dunvegan,—part of Rum,—part of Rasay, and a vast deal of the isle of Sky."

In Sleat, almost all the volcanic strata have been worn away, exposing much older rocks. Extensive areas of dark red sandstone occur in the northern part of the peninsula, and compose the group of rounded heights above Kyleakin clothed with birch and heather, through which protrude great faces of ice-smoothed rock. These hills are in a lonely corner of Skye, but they look down on the busy Kyles to the east and on the series of straits and sounds between Skye, its satellite islands and the mainland. In the west cluster the Red Hills, with the spiry Cuillin over them. The vast undulating moors extend southward, rising in parts to low hills dappled with white quartzite like snow. On the east coast, where the Archæan gneiss outcrops, are wooded slopes, and in glens on the western side grow copses of birch and hazel, with a few gnarled oaks that have weathered numberless storms.

The rough moorlands themselves may seem dull, especially the extensive area in the island's centre. Certainly this area has few hills of unusual character, but they, like most moorland summits, provide wide vistas across the surrounding sea and of the wild Cuillin heights. These upland regions, where a few timid red-deer

roam, are sometimes dappled with changing patterns of cloud shadows. At most seasons they are brightened by flowers, whose perfumes mingle with the incense-like aroma of bog-myrtle. Primroses, violets, pink and white orchids and the insect-collecting, star-leaved Pingucula or bog violet; also yellow potentilla, milkwort as blue as the clear sky, golden whin and purple heather are found in their season. In early summer, the croziers of bracken unfurl their yellow-green fronds. The cotton grass waves its white tufts in boggy places and by lochans in which water-lilies and sweet-scented bog bean bloom in late summer. Many joyful sounds may be heard—the solitary piping of birds, the lark's song, and rushing waters where burns descend from the hills in foaming cascades. Beautiful waterfalls occur in many other places, including Coire na Creiche and the Banachdich burn below the Cuillin. The Ghreadaidh burn has a series of falls through narrow gorges, with birch and rowan springing from clefts in their sheer walls.

The hills and mountains are not the only features of the island's scene, though, as cloud gatherers, they are partly responsible for Skye's Norse derivation from "Ski" (cloud) and "Ey" (island). The colloquial Gaelic name is Eilean Sgiathanach (Winged Island), derived from the Old-Celtic (pre-Norse) "Skeitos" (a wing). These wings are the great storm-beaten promontories that give the island such a long and rugged coastline, with no spot more than 4 miles from the sea. This grand coastline includes magnificent scenery that is much less known than the hills.

The coast generally is low, the high moorland sloping down to low cliffs, or flat ground shelving to narrow, stony beaches. In a few places, however, there are stupendous cliffs, rising at Talisker and Waterstein Head to over 900 feet, and to 1,000 feet or more at Dunvegan Head. These are the greatest sections of bedded basalt in the British Isles, each layer betokening an eruption of molten rock. The whole western coastline of Duirinish, from Dunvegan Head southward, is one vast wall, almost unbroken except by a small sea-loch.   Numerous burns cascade through gorges or plunge over these precipices into the sea.   In tempests, the falling water is dashed from side to side like a writhing serpent or is flung high into the air.   At Talisker, streams tumble over a similar mural escarpment pierced by the glen's mouth.   The foot of this glen is very low, marshy ground flanked by extremely steep hillsides, that make, as it were, a great gateway to the western ocean, guarded by rock stacks in the bay.   Mighty billows thunder on the exposed shore, but in the green glen there is comparative peace.

The Trotternish coast is typical, with lines of low cliffs broken by coves and several fine bays.   On the west side are the open expanse of Score Bay, and the grand horse-shoe bay of Uig surrounded by steep slopes ending in sheer cliffs.   The east side has the beautiful bay of Staffin, with an island and white sands.   South of it are cliffs of prismatic basalt, similar to the pillars of Staffa, and of the Giant's Causeway in Northern Ireland, set above yellow sandstone that is stratified horizontally.   The grandest portion is the Kilt Rock, near which the stream from the freshwater Loch Mealt falls over the cliff's edge.   The prismatic basalt sill caps the whole of the eastern sea-cliffs of Trotternish.   North of Portree the land mounts into a high ridge that falls away very steeply, though not precipitously, as the Portree Cliffs.   From the sea, these cliffs seem to be almost a replica of the lofty escarpment of Beinn Storr.

Perhaps the most unusual low sea-cliffs in the island occur at Glasnakille near Elgol.   Here, cliffs of brown sandstone, about 100 feet high, are eroded horizontally like vast stacks of papers, with copses on their sheltered tops.   These dark walls are broken by deep fissures, originally filled with volcanic rock.   At the head of one fern-draped cleft is the Spar Cave.   This was the retreat of the Episcopal clergyman, Neil MacKinnon who was the first Protestant preacher in this neighbourhood.   When he was ordained in the year 1627, he took a " grite and solemn oathe that he sal treulie, according to his knowledge, gif up to the Clerk of Counsell

20

the names of all Papists knew within the Ilis." The cavern is hollowed out of a thick seam of limestone, and was once noted for its stalactites and stalagmites, described (as well as Loch Coruisk) by Sir Walter Scott in his "Lord of the Isles." It is still lined with a very smooth, milky deposit, and has several limpid pools. West of Elgol are several sea-caves, one of which was a hiding-place of Bonnie Prince Charlie.

An unusual feature of the coastline is the little L-shaped and hammer-headed promontories with narrow isthmuses. The finest are Aird of the Braes opposite Raasay and Ardmore in Vaternish. Near the latter a clan battle was fought in 1580 A.D. between MacDonalds and MacLeods, after the burning alive of a MacLeod congregation in Trumpan Church. A similar headland is Rudha Hunish, the northern tip of Trotternish and Skye itself. From the higher Meall Tuath, this neck of land can be seen, exposed to the full fury of the waves. Westward across the Minch the Outer Hebridean hills rise above lochs and islands. Nearby is Trodday (Island with Pasture), and beyond it, the shadowy mainland fades northward to the Summer Isles and Sutherland heights.

The islands around the Skye coast enhance the variety and beauty of the seascapes. Most of them are small and the home only of seabirds and seals. Loch Bracadale has several isles with cliffs, caves and natural arches, but grass and bracken cover the low islets of Loch Dunvegan. Loch Snizort has the rocky Ascrib Isles, and in the Minch, a few miles north-west of Duntulm, is the group of Fladda Chuain (Fladda of the Ocean). These islands were the site of an early Christian church and burial-ground. Later, they were the safe hiding-place for the title deeds of the MacDonald chief during the 1715 Rising. They were to have been a refuge for Prince Charlie after Culloden, but instead the Prince was fated to wander through Skye.

Off the east coast of Skye lies a chain of larger isles—Rona (Rough Island), uninhabited except for the lighthouse on its northern point; Raasay, the largest one; Scalpay, with its House and sheep-farm; and flat Pabbay, noted for its fossils and rich pasture. Raasay (The Island of Ridges) has much high moorland which in late summer is a mass of purple heather. A prominent landmark is the flat-topped hill, Dun Caan. Boswell, during his sojourn at Raasay House with Samuel Johnson, twice climbed this hill and danced a reel on its summit. He describes it in his Journal: " The ascent to it is by consecutive risings, if that expression may be used when vallies intervene, so that there is but a short rise at once; but it is certainly very high above the sea. The palm of altitude is disputed for by the people of Rasay and those of Sky; the former contending for Dun Can, the latter for the mountains in Sky, over against it." The height of Dun Caan is only 1456 feet, but, because of the approach to it and the wide views it affords, it might be a far loftier eminence. Many of the Outer Hebrides, part of Loch Bracadale, and MacLeod's Tables can be seen over Skye, and to the east is a vast panorama of mainland mountains.

In Loch Scavaig is Soay, once the home of a native breed of sheep. This low island is almost divided in the centre by two small sea-lochs, one of them serving as a natural harbour. From the southern Cuillin on a calm, sunny day, its moors are emerald in a sapphire setting. Boats in the tiny harbour and the cottages near it look like toys, while an excursion steamer heading up Loch Scavaig seems hardly to ruffle the placid waters. The cuckoo calling from the island, brings to mind Wordsworth's lines :

> . . . . the Cuckoo-Bird,
> Breaking the silence of the seas
> Among the farthest Hebrides.

The many sea-lochs of Skye add variety to its grand coastline. They are generally small, of tapering design, and lead in from the open sea or large bays. The big bays are called lochs, the largest being Loch Snizort (Split Firth), with its head divided into Lochs Greshornish and Snizort Beag. The beauty of the fleecy cloud-mountains and of the sunsets which are reflected by such lochs is indescribable. These sunsets recall the Celtic legend in which the dead find themselves on a western shore facing the setting sun, whence they are carried over the gilded waters to Tir nan Og (Land of the Young of Heart), or Tir na Sorcha (Land of Light).

Loch Bracadale on the western seaboard is undoubtedly the most beautiful of the sea-lochs. It is a great bay, almost encircled by land that extends long fingers, ending in islands, into its waters. The bays thus formed, are lochs with different names, the largest of which is Loch Harport. The Cuillin frown upon this long and sinuous arm of the sea, but Loch Beag, adjoining its mouth, is set among the crags and steep slopes of the moorland hills. Loch Bracadale is cradled among these terraced hills that culminate in MacLeod's Tables to the north-west. Even the islands in the loch show the same terraced features, clothed with bright green verdure and rising to cliffs on the seaward side. A line of lofty cliffs ends at Idrigill, the northern outpost of the loch, with below it, great caves and the weird rock pillars—the MacLeod's Maidens. It is to all these diverse features of its broken coastline, and to the moorland hills, that Loch Bracadale owes much of its charm.

Other sea-lochs are miniature fiords, such as Lochs Ainort and Sligachan among the Red Hills. In still weather they too have reflections—of shaggy slopes. They also mirror seabirds that swoop and glide above them, with outspread wings translucent against the blue. In tempests, the heights are lost in swirling cloud from which rain pours in driven blasts. The gale rushing down the glens whips the crests from great waves and lashes the water into a seething turmoil.

The head of Loch Scavaig is a fiord among the southern Cuillin. Here, the peaks of Gars-Bheinn and Sgurr na Stri, like the Torridon mountains of which A. C. Swinburne wrote in one of his most musical poems, tower directly out of the sea :

23

THE SKYE SCENE

The very sea: no mountain-moulded lake
Whose fluctuant shapeliness is fain to take
Shape from the steadfast shore that rules it round,
And only from the storms a casual sound:
The sea, that harbours in her heart sublime
The supreme heart of music deep as time,
And in her spirit strong
The spirit of all imaginable song.

Near the shore at the head of the loch, white sand occurs in patches, partially exposed at low tide like snow against the glaciated rock. The dark waters are glaucous above this white floor, and so clear are they that, in the calmest weather, a boat seems to be floating upon glass of the palest green. Crabs, too, can be distinctly seen through five fathoms, crawling on the bottom. Nearby, oyster-catchers and red-shanks pipe among seaweeds on the rocky shore.

Machair, or the coastal plain formed of fertile calcareous soils resulting from the binding of sand by marram grass, so common in the Outer Hebrides, is not common in Skye. It can be found by a few open bays, whose gracefully curved shores are such a delightful feature of the island's seascapes. At Camasunary (Bay of the White Shieling) by Loch Scavaig is *machair*, with fine level turf that is the happy playground of rabbits and good grazing for sheep.

In the south-east of the island are the straits dividing Skye from the mainland—the Kyles of Akin (or Loch Alsh) and Rhea. Kyle Akin is the Strait of Haco, the Norse king, who moored his galleys here whilst on his way to defeat at the Battle of Largs in the year 1263. Beside the Strait, and the Skye hamlet of the same name, is the gaunt ruin of Castle Maol. By tradition, a toll was levied by the owners of this castle on all passing ships. Kyle Rhea, farther south, is a narrower strait between barren steeps, and is the scene of a great tidal race. Against the flood tide only larger ships may pass, for the swift currents eddy and swirl in miniature whirl-pools so that the dark waters seem to boil. The chief land-route from the island to the distant markets formerly crossed this strait, cattle and horses being towed across it at slack water.

The crofts, or small farms, and straggling townships of Skye have a beauty all their own. The crofters' homes, each standing on its own patch of ground, are small, stone-built structures, with their upper storey set in the roof in order to save space and avoid wind-catching height. Among them are still numbers of the earlier, single-storied dwellings, with dry-stone or roughly cemented walls, and thatched roofs held down by ropes or net weighted with stones. Many of these buildings, that seem to have grown out of the moor, now serve as storeplaces or byres for the cattle. Around them are frequently a few small elders and rowans, supposedly planted as a charm against the Evil-One. Their clusters of white flowers and the berries which follow later, together with the wealth of flowers in the tiny fields, more than compensate for lack of artificial gardens. Large kingcups and bluebells often form carpets of gold and blue. Pink orchids and blue milkwort are followed by the rich flame of birds'-foot trefoil and yellow flags in wayside marshes. Purple and white clover, blue hairbells, scabious and many other flowers bloom among the hayfield grasses.

The crofts are generally separated by fences, and occasionally by stone or turf walls, but the little fields are unenclosed. In them is grown a small quantity of oats, potatoes and sometimes turnips. The oats, like the hay, are mown with the scythe at harvest time and tied into sheaves by hand; the oatfields sometimes being barely 10 yards square. At this season, the crofts look strangely diminutive but homely, with their patchwork of green and golden fields dotted with stooks, above the vast plains of ocean, or against a background of savage peaks. The white-walled cottages nestle under the hill for shelter, peat smoke from them scenting the cool, clear air. In places where the crofts are unfenced, the cows may be tethered to stakes driven in the ground. Not infrequently a cow will drag up the stake and wander away, the crofter's wife crying (or cursing!) in

Gaelic as she chases it, or sends her black and white collie to drive it back. Gaelic is widely spoken among these friendly and hospitable people, but all speak a very pure English.

The island's capital and only town is Portree or Port-an-Righ —the King's Port, its name recalling James V.'s visit in 1540 A.D. to quell the insurgent clansmen of the West Highlands and Islands. It is situated beside a little sea-loch carved out by an Ice-Age glacier from the Cuillin. This loch serves as an excellent natural harbour, with the quay in the shelter of a little tree-clad headland which forms two small bays. Above and around these bays, the stone-built houses cluster among trees. Of recent years the little town has expanded, and now possesses a tweed-mill, and a senior school, with a large hostel for boys, which serves the whole island and some of the Outer Hebrides.

The island people, mostly crofters, now live like those in any other remote rural area in the British Isles. The croft (with its house), for which they pay a low annual rent, provides much of their livelihood, but some supplementary occupation is often necessary. The population of about 9,000 remains fairly constant, though many young people still move to the mainland and its cities to find more profitable employment. Apart from those engaged in the usual community services, many of the islanders are cattle-breeders and shepherds, a few are fishermen and foresters, others cater for visitors in the season, and some of them weave homespuns on handlooms. A small whisky distillery is situated at Carbost by Loch Harport. Below the eastern escarpment of the Trotternish ridge are shallow lochs with beds of diatomite, an ooze formed of millions of flinty algæ-skeletons which show exquisitely beautiful structures under the microscope. These deposits are worked from time to time for manufacture into fine abrasives and other products.

The climate, though including glorious spells of clear sunshine, is generally wet and windy, with more rainy days than most parts of the British Isles. Thus, the weather, combined with the isolation, makes life rather grim for the crofter. However, he is his own master, his living though not easy is secure, and his children receive a sound education. An electricity supply is soon to be carried to all parts of the island. The long winter evenings are pleasantly passed with frequent social-gatherings or *ceilidh* (pronounced kaylee), when songs are sung and stories told around the fireside. Many of these tales have been handed down from generation to generation, though now less cherished than of yore. They tell of the fisherman who married a seal-woman, of the dreaded water horses and bulls that lure people into dark lochans, of kelpies and other devilish sprites, and of fairies dwelling in moorland knolls. The Jacobites and their cause play no small part.

The relics of many bygone peoples are scattered throughout the island, the most important being the ruins of churches, duns and castles. Prehistoric remains are very scanty. Standing stones can be found in several places, the last survivals of dolmen or, as at Uig, of stone circles. In Trumpan churchyard is one of the few mono-liths, like the stone circles and dolmen, a monument or place of worship and sacrifice to the dead. Burial tumuli were also raised, fine examples being three great heaps of boulders near the road south of Dunvegan. Beehive cells, earth houses and other small dwellings are occasionally discovered, but in a poor state. North of Uig, at Kilmuir, the debris of many beehive huts in a Celtic monastery is strewn over what was once an island in a shallow loch. Boulders incised with Pictish symbols of unknown meaning and purpose have been found in Skye, which was held by the Picts until about 670 A.D. These stones are thought to mark the boundaries of church lands, but have no recognised marks of Christianity. One such stone is kept in Dunvegan Castle, another is Clach Ard near Skeabost, and two more remain in situ on Raasay.

No ancient churches or chapels in the island are now used, but the ruins of several mediaeval ones can be seen. They were small structures, with thick stone walls pierced by square or lancet windows, gable-ended and roofed with thatch. Those at Kilchrist near Broadford and Kilmuir at Dunvegan show their original form best. On a tiny island in the river at Snizort near Skeabost is an ancient graveyard. In it are the ruins of two churches, the smaller of which was founded by St. Columba who visited Skye in the 6th century. By deserted Loch Caroy in Bracadale is the ruin of one of the more recent churches—St. John's, standing among wind-swept trees.

The heaped stone ruins of duns (brochs and hill-forts) are now very fragmentary. They were built, on good vantage and easily defended points near the coast, as a defence against Norse invaders in the 9th and 10th centuries. Their Norse names, and those of many place names, are evidence of Norse rule, which gave place to that of the MacLeods in 1280 A.D. The MacLeods built the castle at Dunvegan, and held control of most of the island north of the Cuillin during the following period of clan feuds in the Highlands and Islands. Here, these were against the MacDonalds of Sleat— " Lords of the Isles," and involved the MacKinnons of Strath (between Sleat and the Cuillin).

During this period of clan strife, castles were built to guard each chief's domain, and lands were frequently lost and rewon. These castles were erected by the coast, usually on the sites of duns, the sea serving for protection and communications. Five of them now remain (omitting Dunvegan Castle which is inhabited), with bare, crumbling walls open to the sky, walls that have held many dark deeds and plots, a few of which have come down to us in tradition. Duntulm Castle, a mediaeval stronghold of the MacDonalds of the Isles, is typical. This fortress was defended by sea-cliffs and, on the landward side, by an outer wall and ditch across the little head-land. In its dungeons, about the year 1580, perished Uisdean (or Hugh) MacGhilleasbuig after suffering great torments of hunger and thirst aggravated by salted victuals. Hugh was a cruel and vicious man of great strength and, for his protection, had built himself a castle—Castle Uisdean, a few miles south of Uig. Here, he plotted the death of his kinsman, Donald Gorm Mor, chief of the MacDonalds of Sleat, but the note to the assassin fell into the hands of Donald, who seized and disposed of his enemy.

On the west coast of Sleat is another MacDonald castle, Dunscaith, on the site of the earlier dun of Sgathaich, a warrior queen of the 5th century according to Celtic lore. She taught the arts of war to an almost mythical Irish prince, Cuchullainn, whose deeds have become woven into saga. The Cuillin may derive their name from this culture-hero.

Dunvegan Castle, founded upon a rock by a small inlet of Loch Dunvegan (or Loch Follart), is the greatest and most renowned of all the Hebridean fortresses. It is one of the oldest inhabited castles in Scotland, and is still the home of the head family of Clan MacLeod, as it has been continuously since the first chief, Leod, in the late 13th century. The earliest existing parts including the Water Gate, once the only entrance, were probably built then, on the site of a dun after which it is named (Fort of Becan). During the ages, many additions and alterations have been made, but much of its original starkness is retained. Its massive walls have witnessed many stirring events, but history has noted only a few of them. In the mid-16th century a treacherous chief had a party of Campbells massacred at a feast. On more joyful occasions, its halls must have echoed with song, and the music of harp and bagpipes. Dr. Johnson with Boswell and, later, Sir Walter Scott were entertained here. It now houses a fine collection of historic treasures.

A most cherished possession of the MacLeods is the Fairy Flag, probably a relic from the Crusades adopted as the chief's standard. It is a very delicately woven fragment of amber silk worked with red spots, and is now very tattered. There are several legends about its origin. In all of them it is a gift of the fairies and, when unfurled on three occasions in battle, has the power of increasing the MacLeod's numbers in the eyes of their enemies. It is said to have been used twice with success. Another heirloom is Rorie Mor's drinking-horn, a large ox-horn with silver-work around its mouth. A more interesting relic is the Dunvegan Cup, a communion cup of Irish origin, with a richly ornamented 15th century silver mount, once studded with jewels, in which is a much more ancient mazer, probably of bog-oak. Other treasures include a restored set of MacCrimmon bagpipes, Rory Mor's gourd, a massive carved sideboard dated 1606, a lock of Prince Charlie's hair and his brocaded waistcoat, Flora MacDonald's stays, a great claymore and other weapons, coats óf chain mail, and relics from St. Kilda and other lands. The many documents preserved in the Muniment Room provide a unique account of social conditions in the Hebrides since the 15th century.

The grounds of Dunvegan Castle, like those of most large houses in the island, are now planted with trees. Armadale Castle, an early 19th century pseudo-Gothic mansion and the home of the MacDonalds of Sleat, is similarly situated among woods. Fine old ash and lime trees and lofty silver-firs grow around the house, that overlooks an extensive lawn and faces the mountainous mainland across the Sound of Sleat.

There are two historical houses of which only the foundations now remain—Kingsburgh in west Trotternish, and the House of Coire Chatachan (Corrie of the Wild Cat) below the Red Hills near Broadford. At the latter, generations of MacKinnons offered warm-hearted hospitality to travellers. Dr. Johnson and Boswell were, for a long time, storm-stayed within its shelter. Old Kingsburgh House, near its 19th century successor by Loch Snizort Beag, is named like Portree after James V, and it may have been his residence during his visit in 1540 A.D. The ill-fated Prince Charlie, whilst on his way to Portree with Flora MacDonald, stayed a night at the house which became the home of Flora in the later years of her life. Here, she entertained Samuel Johnson, who slept in the same bed as that occupied by the Prince 37 years earlier. In his " Journey to the Western Islands of Scotland," Johnson later wrote the worthy tribute to her which is inscribed below the huge white Iona cross over her grave in the windswept burial-ground at Kilmuir, Trotternish: " A name that will be mentioned in history, and if courage and fidelity be virtues, mentioned with honour."

The Hebrideans, it should be borne in mind, were not a barbarous people engaged merely in clan feuds, but a highly civilised people, to whom we owe some of the greatest native artistic achievements within the British Isles—their Gaelic poetry and grand pipe-music (*piobaireachd*), the result of centuries of culture. In recent times, these have been robbed of much of their value by translation and adaptation in an effort to romanticise them and increase their popularity. Skye was the home of two families of pipe-musicians— the MacArthurs of Kilmuir near Duntulm, and the renowned MacCrimmons, hereditary pipers to the MacLeods. The MacCrimmons once established a famous school of piping at Boreraig by Loch Dunvegan, at which every would-be piper was required to learn by heart some 200 works to complete his years of training. They also composed many outstanding pibrochs. No doubt the glory of these works was largely inspired by the island's scenery, and the changing effects of colour, light and atmosphere.

As may be apparent, the Skye scene is wonderfully varied, and, in making the effort necessary for its full enjoyment, the visitor will find healthy exercise for the body, refreshment for the spirit and new treasures to enrich the mind.

This Land of Rainbows spanning glens whose walls,
Rock-built, are hung with rainbow-coloured mists
Of far-stretched Meres whose salt flood never rests
Of tuneful Caves and playful Waterfalls
Of Mountains varying momently their crests
Proud be this Land! whose poorest huts are halls
Where fancy entertains becoming guests;
While native song the heroic Past recalls.

WILLIAM WORDSWORTH

AT ISLE ORNSAY, SLEAT

IN brilliant sunshine between passing showers, the white-walled inn stands out among the green fields. On the right is part of Ornsay or the Tidal Island, that makes a sheltered anchorage for the boats of fishermen along this coast. Beyond this natural harbour are the hills above Kyle Rhea.

A CROFT, ISLE ORNSAY

THE crofter's boat, possibly used in connection with lobster fishing, can be seen drawn up on the beach before his cottage. Over the clifftop is Ornsay lighthouse on an islet by the Sound of Sleat. Behind it rise the clouded mainland mountains.

DUNG SLEDGING, FERINDONALD, SLEAT

Fertile ground has earned this eastern seaboard the title of the "Garden of Skye." The panorama it affords of the mainland mountains, among them shapely Ben Sgriol, is one of the glories of Sleat.

POTATO PLANTING

The crofter, with his bag of seed-potatoes slung from his neck, sets them with the wooden dibble.

THE RED HILLS, BROADFORD

BROADFORD with Breakish is the largest crofting township in the island, and extends round a wide bay facing the hills of Applecross. The prominent Red Hill is Beinn na Caillich—Hill of the Old Woman, named according to tradition after a Norse princess who was buried on its summit.

THE RED HILLS

Looking south across the mouth of Loch Ainort from the Portree road, the hills are Beinn na Caillich (left), Beinn Dearg Mhor, Beinn na Cro and Glas Beinn Mhor.

BEN MEABOST, ELGOL

A typical moorland hill with crags on its southern face. The wide views it presents of mountains, sea-lochs and islands compose a magnificent panorama.

A HARVEST SCENE AT TORRIN

At the western foot of the Red Hills is the crofting hamlet of Torrin, which has a magnificent mountain background in Blaven and its adjoining summits. The great cleft head of this gabbro mountain (left) and the riven crags of the Clach Glas ridge to its north tower above the bird-haunted head of Loch Slapin, near which Torrin is situated. The lighter hill is Sgurr nan Each (The Notched Peak) in front of Garbh-bheinn or the Rough Hill. In the foreground can be seen the handle of the scythe used for cutting the oats. After they have been bundled into sheaves, the oats are placed in stooks. Frequently, as here, a sheaf is bound over the top of each stook as protection from rain and high winds. The low and rounded haystacks, likewise, have a patch of canvas sheeting over their crown, and are tied or weighted down.

BLAVEN FROM KILBRIDE

" At a clear open bend in the road
My passion went up in a cry,
For the wonderful mountain of Blaavin
Was bearing his huge bulk on high. . . ."

ALEXANDER SMITH.

CAMASUNARY AND BLAVEN FROM BEN CLEAT

STRATH Creitheach or the Vale of Brushwood, that ends at Camasunary by Loch Scavaig, is part of the valley dividing the Cuillin from the Red Hills and Blaven. The igneous rocks of which these widely differing hills are built meet in Marsco, the shapely hill over Loch Creitheach, where the granite has invaded the gabbro and produced a unique and very hard rock, exposed as crags on the upper slopes. Adjoining Marsco is Ruadh Stac or the Rosy Pile, facing dark Sgurr Hain and farther Sgurr nan Gillean. On the right, Blaven raises its lofty head above the riven flanks of its long south-west ridge, an easy route to the summit. The moorland hill in the foreground has been rounded by ice action, but it still clearly shows the strange terraces characteristic of the bedded-basalt slopes.

THE RED HILLS FROM BEN MEABOST

SHADOWY Beinn na Cro and the twin domes of Beinn Dearg are among the most shapely of the Red Hills. Kilmarie Lodge is set among trees in the cloud-shadowed moorland.

THE CUILLIN FROM BEN CLEAT, ELGOL

HAIL showers sweep over the Cuillin, and veil Marsco (right) beyond Camasunary or the Bay of the White Shieling. A glimpse can be had of Loch Coruisk amid the mountains.

A COTTAGE AT ELGOL

THIS cottage, like most houses in the island, has no ornamental
garden, but the multitude of hayfield flowers and the wide views
are more than compensation. Above Loch Scavaig looms the Cuillin
peak, Gars-bheinn, like the gnomen of a gigantic sundial.

THE CUILLIN FROM ELGOL

THE Cuillin across Loch Scavaig give Elgol a superb mountain outlook that is unique in the British Isles. The dark peak on the right is Sgurr na Stri (1623 ft.), the fine near view-point for these mountains. The slopes of this bare hill have been steepened and smoothed by Ice Age glaciers that passed over and around it. Its name means the Peak of Contention, perhaps because it stood on the boundary between the lands of MacLeod and MacKinnon, or because it is cleft by an eroded dyke of intrusive rock that divides its summit into two parts of almost equal height. The little fishing craft can be moored in the bay for only about three months of the year because of the sudden squalls that sweep Loch Scavaig, the Norsemen's Bay of Destruction.

RHUM FROM BEN CLEAT

THE nearest Hebridean island to Skye seen over the crofting township of Elgol. The wild outline of its peaks are a fascinating feature from almost anywhere in southern Skye, but the island is a strictly preserved deer forest.

EIGG FROM THE HEAD OF LOCH SCAVAIG

OVER the rocky islet to the right are the peaks of Rhum, with the Isle of Muck between it and Eigg. The boulders on the shore lie beside the rock shelf known as the " Bad Step," that is on the track around Sgurr na Stri. The boat is bringing visitors to Loch Coruisk.

THE " DUBHS RIDGE " AND HEAD OF LOCH SCAVAIG

WHITE sand changes the clear sea-water here to a pale green. A few rowans grow among great boulders by the shore and in one spot, primroses, violets and orchids bloom amid brambles and bracken. The corrie to the left of the " Dubhs Ridge " is the Rough Corrie or An Gharbh-choire.

LOCH CORUISK AND THE CUILLIN FROM SGURR NA STRI

THE peaks encircling the loch are "The Dubhs" (left), Sgurr Mhic Coinnich, Sgurr Dearg crowned by its "Inaccessible" Pinnacle, Sgurr na Banachdich, Sgurr a' Ghreadaidh, Sgurr Mhadaidh and Bidein at the end of its ridge—Druim nan Ramh. This ridge divides Coir' Uisg with its loch from Harta Corrie below the northern Cuillin, and, like Sgurr na Stri, has been steepened and smoothed by glaciers from the local ice-cap over these mountains in the Ice Age. The ice also gouged out the basin of the loch, whose surface is but 26 feet above sea-level, to a depth of over 120 feet. The imposing outline of the peaks and the rich shades of the bare rock, in contrast to the lighter tones of the loch and the pool of brilliant green at its head, compose a scene of sombre magnificence; one that is a masterpiece of Nature.

THE NORTHERN CUILLIN FROM SGURR NA STRI

OVER sunlit Harta Corrie and the pyramid of Sgurr na h-Uamha or Peak of the Cave are the snowy summit of Bruach na Frithe, dark Am Basteir and spiry Sgurr nan Gillean.

THE SOUTHERN CUILLIN FROM SGURR NA STRI

GARS-BHEINN (2934 ft.), Sgurr a' Choire Bhig and Sgurr nan Eag (3037 ft.) tower above the head of Loch Scavaig, into which falls the outflow from Loch Coruisk (right). A number of streams cascade down the mountain side after rain, one of them from An Gharbh-choire known as the Mad Burn or Allt a' Chaoich.

LOOKING NORTH FROM SGURR NAN EAG

SGURR Alasdair and Sgurr Thearlaich rise over the sunlit head of Coir' a' Ghrunnda. On the right, above An Gharbh-choire, is Sgurr Dubh na Da Bheinn (3069 ft.), with distant Sgurr na Ghreadaidh behind it. The dark mass of rock above Coir' a' Ghrunnda is the Castle or Caisteal a' Gharbh-choire.

SGURR ALASDAIR OVER LOCH COIR' A' GHRUNNDA

THIS loch, in one of the finest Cuillin corries, is 2300 feet above sea-level, and has patches of brown sand on its edge, worn from iron-bearing rock. North of the loch tower Sgurr Sgumain (left), the pyramid of Sgurr Alasdair—the highest Cuillin peak (3251 ft.), and pointed Sgurr Thearlaich (3201 ft.).

SGURR SGUMAIN FROM SGURR DEARG (WEST RIDGE)

THE Great Stone Shoot drops below Sgurr Alasdair into the depths of Coire Lagan, with its dark lochan beneath the shadowy crags of Sgurr Sgumain (3104 ft.), above which peeps farther Sgurr nan Eag (3037 ft.). On the cliff face of Sron na Ciche (right), noted for its rock climbs, is the shadow of the huge rock boss—The Cioch or Breast.

SGURR NA GHREADAIDH FROM SGURR DEARG (WEST RIDGE)

BEYOND Sgurr na Ghreadaidh (3190 ft.) are Sgurr a' Mhadaidh, lighter Bruach na Frithe, and cleft Am Basteir. These peaks, seen over the Bealach or Pass of Coire Banachdich between Sgurr na Banachdich and Sgurr Dearg (right), clearly show the inclination of the intrusive sills upward from the Coruisk Basin.

THE WESTERN CUILLIN ABOVE GLEN BRITTLE

THE peaks are Sgurr a' Mhadaidh (left), Sgurr na Ghreadaidh above its corrie, the pinnacle of Sgurr Thormaid, Sgurr na Banachdich over Coir' an Eich and Sgurr nan Gobhar, Sgurr Dearg above Coire Banachdich, and dark Sgurr Alasdair with Sgumain. On the roadside stands the S.Y.H.A. Hostel, by the Coire Ghreadaidh burn with its numerous waterfalls.

EAS MOR, GLEN BRITTLE

THIS fall on the Coire Banachdich burn drops nearly 150 feet into a gorge on the hillside above Glen Brittle House. Some idea of its size is given by the rowan tree on the skyline. Most waterfalls in the island are best seen after rain, as the water soon drains away from the slopes.

EVENING, GLEN BRITTLE

THE shadows of the western hills spread across the valley and up the sides of the Cuillin as the sun sinks. There is an ancient fort on Rudh' an Dunain, the point south of Loch Brittle, over which are the hills of Rhum. Glen Brittle House stands among the trees.

LOCH CORUISK AND BLAVEN FROM SGURR NA BANACHDICH

SNOW dapples the summit of Sgurr Dubh Mor (3089 ft.), beneath which is the pointed top of Sgurr Dubh Beag (2420 ft.). Below is green and grey Coir' Uisg—the Corrie of the Water, with heavily glaciated and precipitous Sgurr na Stri above the end of the loch. Beyond lie Sleat and the mountainous mainland.

COIRE NA CREICHE

THIS corrie is the site of the last Skye clan battle, in 1601 A.D., following a cattle stealing raid. Around it are Bruach na Frithe (left), Sgurr an Fheadain with its Waterpipe Gully, Bidein in cloud, Sgurr a' Mhadaidh and Sgurr Thuilm. The "Waterpipe" is 1309 feet high and is probably the longest gulley in the British Isles.

THE COIRE LAGAN PEAKS FROM SGURR NA BANACHDICH

THE peaks are " The Dubhs " with snow patches, Sgurr Mhic Coinnich, pointed Sgurr Thearlaich and Sgurr Alasdair above the sunlit head of Coire Lagan, and Sgurr Dearg (3210 ft.) topped by the " Inaccessible " Pinnacle, with An Stac in shadow below it. Sgurr na Banachdich (3167 ft.) is easily climbed by Coir' an Eich, and is one of the best Cuillin summits for distant views.

THE WESTERN CUILLIN FROM BRUACH NA FRITHE

ALMOST all the Cuillin peaks are visible from this summit. Here, Gars-bheinn (left), "The Dubhs," Sgurr Alasdair and Sgurr Dearg are seen over Sgurr na Bhairnich (The Limpet Peak), An Caisteal and Bidein Druim nan Ramh. The top of Druim nan Ramh (The Ridge of Oars), that divides the Coruisk Basin from Harta Corrie, is just visible.

BLAVEN FROM BRUACH NA FRITHE

NORTH of Blaven are Clach Glas and Garbh-bheinn above light Ruadh Stac, whose scree-covered top makes a striking contrast with Blaven's bare face of solid rock. Below is Lota Corrie in the head of Harta Corrie, with the dark cone of Sgurr na h-Uamha above it.

SGURR NAN GILLEAN FROM BRUACH NA FRITHE

SGURR nan Gillean provides many rope climbs on its northern Ridge of Pinnacles, and a Tourist Route up its South-East Ridge, though this involves some scrambling. Bruach na Frithe (3143 ft.), however, is an easily accessible Cuillin top from Fionn Choire (The White Corrie), here seen with snow patches at its head.

THE NORTHERN CUILLIN, SLIGACHAN

THE conical peaks are Sgurr nan Gillean (3167 ft.) and, on the right, Sgurr a' Bhasteir or Peak of the Executioner, after the resemblance of a rock pinnacle between the peaks to an axe-head. Sligachan is probably the best centre for the northern peaks of both the Cuillin and Red Hills.

MARSCO ABOVE GLEN SLIGACHAN

This peak among the Red Hills shows the level of the Ice Age glacier that filled the valley. A rough track threads the glen, with the Cuillin, Marsco and Blaven like mighty walls above its boggy floor.

GLAMAIG FROM SLIGACHAN

Glamaig is a ridged hill rising to 2537 feet above the south shore of Loch Sligachan, but from here its end is seen as a great rosy-grey pyramid.

RAASAY FROM SCONSER
  The conical peak is the summit of Dun Caan (Hill of the Broch), and is a remnant of the basalt plateau that forms most of Skye.

THE SOUND OF RAASAY LOOKING NORTH
  The rocky height is Beinn Tianavaig near Portree, with the Storr mountain and Portree Cliffs beyond it. Raasay House stands near the shore by the distant rocky islet (right).

A SKYE COTTAGE

TYPICAL of the earlier kind of dwellings is this one at Luib by Loch Ainort, with its rough stone walls and roof of loose thatch held down by a weighted net. Behind it is the usual cluster of rowans and other small trees. The crofter is bearing home a fleece.

PRESHAL MOR, TALISKER

THIS hill is only 1000 feet in height, yet it is one of the most imposing hills in the island. Talisker House is hidden among the trees, above which is part of Preshal Beag—The Lesser Beacon Mountain. The sheep farm here is one of the most extensive in Skye.

LOCH BRACADALE

LOOKING north from near Fiscavaig, the nearest island in the blue loch is Oronsay. Above the farther shore rise the hills in Duirinish called MacLeod's Tables. After their defeat at the Battle of Largs in 1263 A.D., the Norse fleet with the dying king, Haco, moored in Loch Bracadale to prepare for their homeward voyage.

THE SPINNER

AT Portnalong and Fiscavaig in Minginish are crofters resettled from Harris, who do weaving and knitting in their homes, many of them spinning and sometimes dyeing the wool.

LOCH BEAG, BRACADALE

THE delightfully winding road to Dunvegan follows the shore of this lonely inlet of the sea. From Loch Beag, a road to Portree crosses the moorland heart of the island, uninhabited except for a few crofts in Glen Mor. In Bracadale is the best preserved broch in the island—Dun Beag.

71

MACLEOD'S TABLES FROM BRACADALE

A distant view of these moorland hills over the silvery
waters of Loch Bracadale seen from the Dunvegan road
at Coillore, near Loch Beag.

MACLEOD'S TABLES, DUIRINISH

Seen across the head of Loch Dunvegan, loftier
Healaval Beag or the Lesser Table Mountain (1601 ft.)
rises to the south of its neighbour, Healaval Mor.

THE COAST OF VATERNISH

A PROSPECT at evening overlooking the hamlet of Stein. The farthest headland in strangely-shaped Ard Mor. Stein was founded in 1787 A.D. by the Scottish Fishery Board, who built a pier, stores and houses; but the scheme failed, and the buildings were used for crofters dispossessed by the Clearances.

WATERSTEIN HEAD, DUIRINISH

FROM Eist Head, the most westerly point in the island, this 967 foot cliff dwarfs fishing boats moored in the bay. Beyond it, down the farther cliffs, a stream tumbles over 250 feet straight to the sea. Waterstein, the Prominent Stone or Stone of the Waters clearly shows its structural layers of basalt. At its base, the great sill of columnar basalt underlying all these rocks comes to the surface, and forms the strange promontory of Eist Head. The latter point has, at the narrowest part, a steep hill over 300 feet high that falls away sheer from its summit on the western side. This hill gives the headland its name—Head of the Stallion—from its appearance as seen from the lighthouse, which is the only one on the mainland of Skye.

LOCH DUNVEGAN, ARDMORE, VATERNISH

OVER the placid water rise Beinn Bhreac and distant Healaval Mor above Clett and Mingay. These islands are formed of the same sill of columnar basalt as the Kilt Rock in Trotternish. The rough road leads from Trumpan Church close by.

DUNVEGAN CASTLE—NORTH FACE

"IT looks as if let down from heaven by the four corners to be the residence of a chief"—Boswell. In the unfaced outer wall, built in the 13th century and the oldest existing part of the castle, is the Sea Gate, once the only entrance. A boat was formerly needed to reach the gateway as there was deep seawater at the foot of the rock. On the landward side, the defences were strengthened by a semi-artificial fosse that in the course of time has become partly filled up. The policies are now thickly wooded, conifers on the higher slopes and, near the castle, ash, beech and other deciduous trees among which grow rhododendrons, azaleas, tree-heaths and many other flowering shrubs. In this woodland garden is the fern-fringed waterfall—"Rorie Mor's Nurse"—named after the well-loved laird, Sir Roderick MacLeod.

DUNVEGAN CASTLE—EAST FACE

THE main entrance, battlements and corner turrets are 19th century additions. The 16th century Fairy Tower on the south side, with its crow-stepped gables and embattled parapet, has altered little during the ages.

KILMUIR, DUNVEGAN

This is one of the best preserved of the ancient churches and chapels in the island, all of which are now in ruins.

PLOUGHING AT WATERSTEIN, DUIRINISH

Oats and potatoes, mainly for cattle-feed, are the chief crops. In the background is the freshwater Loch Mor.

MACLEOD'S TABLE NORTH FROM DUNVEGAN

HEALAVAL Mor (1538 ft.) with its "tablecloth." A pleasing tale is told in Skye of an evening banquet held on this hill, to prove to a Lowland courtier that here there are finer tables in more superb surroundings, with the heavens for a roof and torchbearers for sconces.

THE QUAY, PORTREE

THE quay with its picturesque houses is built in the shelter of a little headland called The Meall. On its grassy crown, beside the tower seen above the trees, the annual Skye Gathering is held. Low cloud hides the distant Cuillin, but the slopes of Fingal's Seat—a fine viewpoint—remain clear.

BEN TIANAVAIG, PORTREE

Ben Tianavaig, 1352 feet in height, rises to the east of Loch Portree. Below its northern crags, riddled with sea caves, is the mouth of the loch sheltered by Raasay.

SOMERLED SQUARE, PORTREE

Named after the first " Lord of the Isles," this large square is the hub from which radiate the few narrow streets of the little town. In its centre is the war memorial.

THE ROAD TO THE STORR

THE rock pinnacle known as the Old Man is a prominent landmark below the precipices of this mountain, and is probably best seen from the south near Loch Fada, some three miles north of Portree. Loch Fada (The Long Loch), which lies to the east of the road, is noted for its trout.

THE OLD MAN OF STORR

THE Old Man, about 150 feet high, is the petrified monarch among the rock pinnacles on 2360 feet high Beinn Storr, whose precipices tower high above, black in contrast with the bright green slopes. The heavy raincloud drifting overhead adds to the weird desolation of this place.

ON THE EAST COAST OF TROTTERNISH

THE low headland is Rudha nam Brathairean or Point of the Brothers, a few miles south of Staffin. Across the Sound is Rona or the Rough Island, part of Raasay and the hills of Applecross on the mainland. On such brilliant days as this, the sea is an intense blue.

THE KILT ROCK, EAST TROTTERNISH

THIS rock formation gives the nearby crofting township of Staffin its name—the Place of Pillars. The same sill of prismatic basalt occurs in all the cliffs southward to Portree, though nowhere else is it so perfectly formed or so easily seen from land.

85

STAFFIN AND THE QUIRANG HEIGHTS

THE Quirang is situated among the precipices of the hill on the left, with crofts in Brogaig below it. The tabular hill is Leac na Fionn with Sron Vourlinn, named by tradition after a Norse princess, Biornal. All the fertile ground around the beautiful Bay of Staffin is scattered with crofts.

THE NEEDLE ROCK, THE QUIRANG

ABOVE this rock pillar, about 120 feet high and eroded out of the cliff face, is the hollow called the Quirang or Pit of the Ridge. In it is the Table, a rock platform capped with fine turf. The steep slopes here afford wide views over the sea to the mainland mountains lining the horizon.

87

DUNTULM CASTLE

The ancient stronghold of the MacDonald chiefs, "Lords of the Isles," built on the site of an earlier Celtic fortress. Below the little headland is the cove where the galleys were kept.

CROFTERS AT WORK, STAFFIN

In parts of the island where horses for ploughing are scarce, the arable ground has to be dug. Here, the crofter is dragging a harrow while his family finish the digging.

THE COAST NEAR DUNTULM

THE road northward follows the shore of Score Bay beneath a hill with crumbling crags of poorly formed prismatic basalt. Beyond this hill is Duntulm Castle perched on its headland and, on the horizon, the great columnar cliffs of the Shiant Isles, the home of countless sea-birds.

ROCKS NEAR THE QUIRANG

THESE rocks, that cap a green hillock below the Needle, are called the Prison, Castle and Tower. On the talus slopes grow numerous rock-plants, among them purple saxifrage, and moss campion (silene) with its cushions of rosy flowers in early summer.

THE TROTTERNISH HEIGHTS

LOOKING south from near the Quirang, the light peak in the centre is Beinn Edra (2003 ft.), with Sgurr a' Mhadaidh Ruaidh (The Red Fox's Peak) and the Storr beyond it. Diatomite, used for manufacture into fine abrasives, is obtained from shallow lochs in the boggy moorland below these hills.

PRECIPICES NEAR THE QUIRANG

THE road from Staffin to Uig winds in a great hairpin curve over the eastern escarpment of the Trotternish ridge. Grassy slopes below the crags provide excellent grazing for sheep. The precipices and hillocks here are due to dissolving of the calcareous substrata with subsequent sinking of the heavy basalt rocks.

UIG FROM BRAE CONON

THE finely curved bay at Uig is one of the most beautiful bays in the island and has a perfect setting, with green slopes, dotted with whitewashed cottages, surrounding it like an amphitheatre. Above the bay is Idrigil or the Outer Hill, and across blue Loch Snizort lies Vaternish, the Prominent Headland or Promontory of the Water.

UIG—SOUTH SIDE

HERE are small woods, rare in Skye, at the foot of Glen Conon. A house built as a round tower can be seen on the farther hillside. Near the top of this hill is a Standing Stone, once part of a stone circle, and on a perfect site for such a monument.

UIG FROM IDRIGIL

A POOL of sunlight passes over Uig and the bay, but heavy cloud shrouds Beinn Edra above Glen Conon. On the south side of this glen are masses of rock crowning grassy mounds, similar to those on the other side of the ridge of Trotternish. The largest of these tors is Ewen's Castle.

THE COAST NORTH OF UIG

THE coast near Kilmuir seen from Idrigil. The craggy hill is Dun Skudiburgh, with ruins of an old dun—the Watcher's Fort—on its top. The stack below it resembles those in Loch Bracadale called MacLeod's Maidens. About a mile north of this point, Bonnie Prince Charlie with Flora MacDonald landed in Skye.